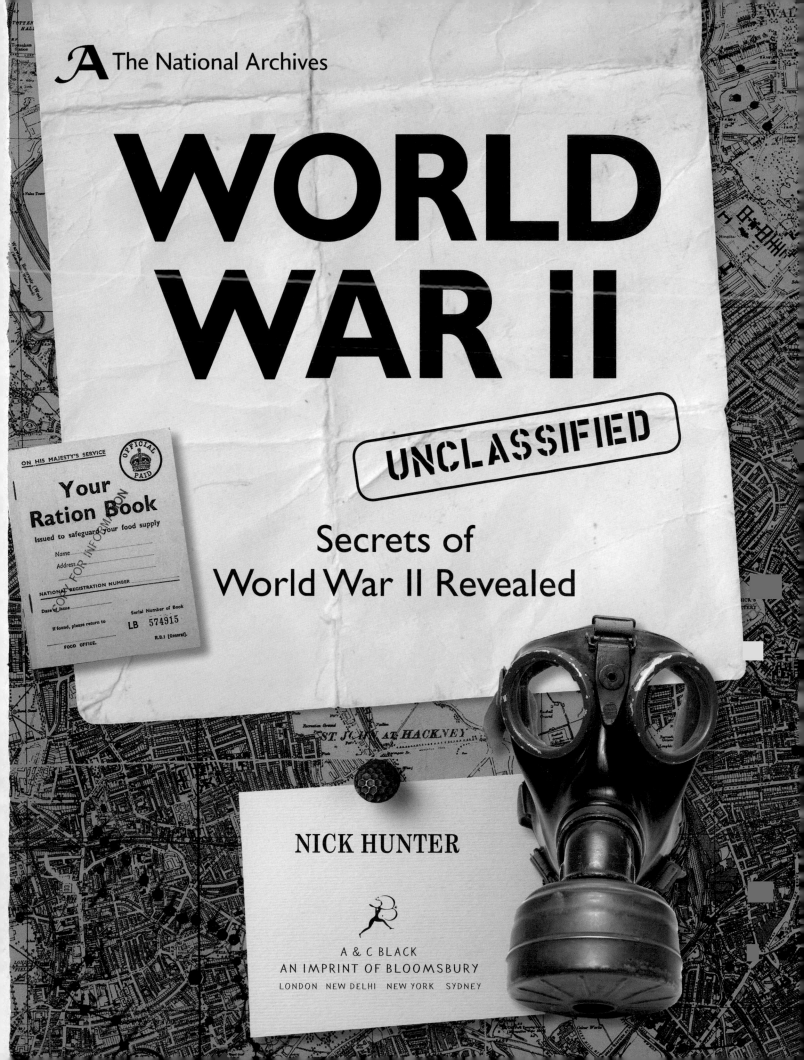

The National Archives

WORLD WAR II

UNCLASSIFIED

Secrets of
World War II Revealed

NICK HUNTER

A & C BLACK
AN IMPRINT OF BLOOMSBURY
LONDON NEW DELHI NEW YORK SYDNEY

Published 2015 by A & C Black,
an imprint of Bloomsbury Publishing Plc,
50 Bedford Square
London, WC1B 3DP

www.bloomsbury.com

Design by Nick Avery Design

ISBN: 978-1-4729-2000-3

A CIP catalogue for this book is available from the British Library.

This book is produced using paper that is made from wood grown in
managed, sustainable forests. It is natural, renewable and recyclable.
The logging and manufacturing processes conform to the environmental
regulations of the country of origin.

Printed in China by Leo Paper Products, Heshan, Guangdong

1 3 5 7 9 10 8 6 4 2

CONTENTS

Storming the Beaches

Under the cover of darkness, a vast fleet of ships crept unseen across the English Channel. When dawn broke on 6 June 1944, otherwise known as D-Day, the ships' guns started a ferocious bombardment of the German defences on the Normandy coast.

As the shells exploded around them, the Germans would have seen the landing craft wallowing in the rough sea. These landing craft carried 133,000 troops from Great Britain, the United States, Canada and many other nations. Their assault would begin the invasion of France and, as they hoped, the eventual defeat of Nazi Germany.

▲ American troops launch themselves against the German defences on D-Day.

The invasion of the Normandy coast had been planned over many months by the leaders and generals of the Allies, which included the United States, Great Britain and Canada. They had hoped to leave nothing to chance, but the invasion had already been delayed by one day because of bad weather. Germany's leader Adolf Hitler believed that his armed forces, which had controlled most of Western Europe since 1940, would repel the invaders. Defeat for either side would mean disaster.

◀ Beyond the Normandy beaches, these paratroops are preparing to be dropped behind enemy lines.

Total war

D-Day was one of the most important days of a conflict that caused more death and destruction than any war in history. World War II's battles and bombing raids raged across Western Europe, Russia, North Africa, Southeast Asia and the world's oceans. By the time of the war's terrible end in the Japanese cities of Hiroshima and Nagasaki, as many as 60 million people had lost their lives. This book uses original and sometimes declassified top-secret documents from The National Archives to tell the story of the heroes and horrors of a war like no other.

WAR DIARY
or
INTELLIGENCE SUMMARY
(Delete heading not required).

Unit........ 4 Commando.

Commanding Officer........ Lt.Col.

Jun 44.

Summary of Events and Information

Lt.Col.R W.P.Dawson moved forward to contact 2nd. Bn East Yorks Regt and was wounded in the head. He was, however, sufficiently able to order the Commando to move off from the Assembly Area, relinquishing command of the Commando when the Second in Command passed him, saying that he intended, if it was possible to follow on behind. The Second in Command ordered the medical orderlies to give him some morphine. Col. Dawson was again seen on the road after the Battery had been taken, he was then sent by the Medical Officer to the BDS. On the evening of D plus 1 (7 Jun 44) Col. Dawson arrived in a Jeep at Commando defence positions at HAUGER, and stayed there until D plus 3 when he was ordered to be evacuated by the ADMS.

'C' Tp waited for the remainder of the Commando to position itself, and then moved on behind 1 and 8 (Fighting Frenchs) Tps along the OUISTREHAM road to the Check Pt, being harrassed by snipers and machine gunners in houses. Tanks greatly helped in clearing this opposition. From the Check Pt, 'C' Tp again took the lead and established a route to the Battery — The Commandos main task. Invaluable assistance was given to the leading Tp by a French Gendarme member of the Underground Movement, who helped the Commando to by pass other enemy strongpoints and reach their objective without unnecessary delay. Great help was also afforded the Unit by 4 Centaurs which gave cover from snipers. On arrival at major tank obstacles covering the inland side of the Battery strongpoint, and still under enemy fire, a search was made and two suitable bridges made. Here, a machine gun post and mortar position were silenced by PIAT fire.

Together with 'A' Tp, under command of Capt A.M.Thorburn, 'C' Tp then gave covering fire to enable 'D' Tp, (commanded by Major P.A.Porteous VC) to pass through 'B' Tp, (commanded by Capt. H.Burt) and 'F' Tp (commanded by Capt. L.N.Coulson), were then covered across. Continued sniping and mortar fire inflicted further casualties.

▲ Plans for D-Day included artificial Mulberry harbours that would be towed into position as bases for unloading tanks and supplies for the invasion force.

HITLER AND THE NAZIS

The spark for World War II lay in the ashes of the previous war, stirred up by a man who claimed he could restore Germany's power. Germany had been blamed for starting World War I in the Treaty of Versailles. The Treaty was a peace settlement dictated by the victors of World War I. Germany had been stripped of territory, forced to dismantle much of her armed forces, and ordered to pay for the cost of the war.

Adolf Hitler fought and was injured in the German army during World War I. However, by 1921 Hitler's extreme views and forceful personality had helped to win him the leadership of the National Socialist German Workers' Party, also called the Nazis.

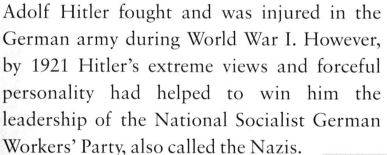

▶ *Hitler's extreme views were set out in his book* Mein Kampf, *meaning* My Struggle, *first published in 1925.*

Hitler's rise to power

Germany had been thrown into economic turmoil by World War I and unemployment soared when an economic crisis hit the world in

▶ *Hitler and the Nazis believed in ruling by force. Once Hitler was in power, he put an end to democratic elections, so the German people could not elect another leader.*

"I am told… that really the most dangerous man of all is the Führer himself. He falls into fits of passion and will listen to no advice… No one wants war; certainly, but when you have a passionate lunatic at the top who still commands the devotion of the populace and who is evidently prepared to run great risks, then already the situation is dangerous."

A secret report to the British government, by businessman Mr Law, who worked in Germany, written in 1937.

1929. The German people looked for someone to blame, and Hitler convinced many that Jews and communists were responsible for Germany's problems. In 1932, the Nazis became the largest party in the German parliament. In January 1933, Hitler became Chancellor of Germany. He ruthlessly attacked all opposition and in August 1934 declared himself Führer, the undisputed leader of Germany.

Nazi beliefs

Hitler preached that the strong German race had been betrayed by others, especially Jews and communists. Hitler's vision of a strong Germany depended on defeating these enemies.

▲ Jews were persecuted by the Nazi regime. They were also forced to wear the Star of David.

THE GATHERING STORM

Hitler preached that only military force could restore Germany's position in the world, lost after World War I came to an end. Many Germans believed that their country had not been defeated in the previous war. Instead, they believed that her military leaders had been "stabbed in the back" by the civilians who had agreed to end the fighting. Hitler immediately started rebuilding the country's military might, which had been forbidden in the Treaty of Versailles.

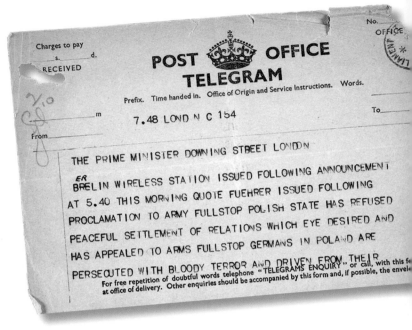

▲ *Veteran British politician, Winston Churchill, was sometimes the only voice warning about Hitler's plans. This telegram, which tells him about the invasion of Poland, shows he had been right all along.*

▲ *When war broke out, people were not surprised. Millions of gas masks had been distributed in September 1938 in case of an enemy gas attack.*

Turbulent times

The 1930s were a violent time in many parts of the world. In 1931, Japan invaded the Chinese region of Manchuria; Italy's dictator Mussolini launched an invasion of Abyssinia, East Africa in 1935; and Spain erupted in civil war between 1936 and 1939, which brought dictator Francisco Franco to power.

In March 1936, Hitler ordered German troops into the land west of the River Rhine, which, according to the Treaty, was supposed to remain free of German troops. Great Britain and France, desperate to avoid another war, did nothing. Hitler then invaded German-speaking Austria on 14 March 1938 and was welcomed by many Austrians.

German minorities also lived in Czechoslovakia and Poland. At the Munich conference in September 1938, Britain and France agreed that Hitler could take over the German-speaking part of Czechoslovakia. The Czech government was not even invited to the conference. In March 1939, Hitler established German rule over most of Czechoslovakia, breaking the agreement made at Munich.

The last chance

Britain and France knew that they had been tricked at the Munich conference and now had no choice but to stop Hitler. The Führer, however, seemed determined on war, helped by an unlikely alliance with the communist Soviet Union. On 1 September 1939, German troops invaded Poland. The western allies protested, but Hitler did not back down. As a result, on 3 September 1939, Britain and France declared war on Germany.

▶ *Neville Chamberlain was British Prime Minister from 1937 until 1940.*

46

We, the German Führer and Chancellor and the British Prime Minister, have had a further meeting today and are agreed in recognising that the question of Anglo-German relations is of the first importance for the two countries and for Europe.

We regard the agreement signed last night and the Anglo-German Naval Agreement as symbolic of the desire of our two peoples never to go to war with one another again.

We are resolved that the method of consultation shall be the method adopted to deal with any other questions that may concern our two countries, and we are determined to continue our efforts to remove possible sources of difference and thus to contribute to assure the peace of Europe.

(Signed) A. HITLER.

(Signed) NEVILLE CHAMBERLAIN.

WWII FACTS

THE MUNICH AGREEMENT

British Prime Minister Neville Chamberlain claimed that this agreement, made at the Munich Conference on 30 September 1938 would mean "peace for our time". Chamberlain's weakness convinced Hitler that he could take whatever he wanted.

▶ *German troops invading Poland during September 1939.*

BLITZKRIEG ACROSS EUROPE

Soon after Neville Chamberlain announced the outbreak of war on the radio, air raid sirens sounded in British cities.

The government expected immediate attack from the air, but this was a false alarm. For most people in Western Europe, nothing much seemed to happen for the first eight months of the conflict, which was called the 'Phoney War'. In Poland things were very different.

▲ Around 340,000 British, French and Belgian troops were evacuated from the beaches of Dunkirk, leaving most of their equipment behind.

Poland's pain

In their invasion of Poland in September 1939, the Nazis unleashed a new kind of assault – Blitzkrieg – meaning lightning war. Dive-bombing aircraft attacked, which knocked out much of the Polish defence. Towns and cities were bombed to create panic and terror. Tanks and infantry advanced quickly into this chaos. On 17 September, the Soviet Union invaded eastern Poland, as part of their treaty with Hitler. The Polish fought bravely but were forced to surrender on 27 September.

War in the west

In April 1940, Hitler's armies marched into Denmark and Norway. On 10 May, the Nazi invasion in the west began. The Netherlands and Belgium were defeated in a few days. The French had built a huge system of fortifications called the Maginot Line to prevent German invasion.

▼ British forces had been cut off by the German advance. They were forced to flee to the coast, where a fleet of large and small ships rescued them.

German forces simply concentrated their attacks either side of the line, cutting off the French defenders. On 22 June, an agreement to end the fighting, called an armistice, was put in place, giving Germany control of northern and western France. A puppet government, forced to follow Hitler's orders, would rule from Vichy in the south of France.

With victory seemingly assured, Italy, led by Benito Mussolini, joined the war on Germany's side. Britain stood alone. Could it avoid the same fate as France?

▼ *Adolf Hitler visits Paris in triumph after the defeat of France.*

BATTLE OF BRITAIN

Winston Churchill took over from Neville Chamberlain as British prime minister in May 1940. Churchill told Parliament that he had "nothing to offer but blood, toil, tears and sweat". Britain was in great danger. The defeat of France gave Hitler a base a few miles away from which he could launch an invasion.

Britain prepared to defend itself. Groups of Local Defence Volunteers, who were too old to join the armed forces or working in protected jobs, were formed. Lines of protection such as trenches and barbed wire were built to try and slow down the invading forces.

Battle in the air

But no invasion could be launched until the Royal Air Force (RAF) had been defeated. From August 1940, wave after wave of German fighter aircraft tried to defeat the Spitfires and Hurricanes of the Royal Air Force. Radar technology was used to warn the British pilots of German attacks. Pilots could be in the air within a few minutes. The German air force, known as the Luftwaffe, tried to bomb the airfields of southern England, but they failed to do enough damage to tip the balance in their favour. After a final effort on 15 September 1940, plans for invasion were cancelled. Britain was saved, for now.

▲ Winston Churchill's defiant speeches, radio broadcasts, and his refusal to consider defeat, inspired the British people through the darkest days of 1940.

▼ *The Royal Air Force lost 915 aircraft during the Battle of Britain, but factories produced 500 new aircraft every week.*

▼ *The 2940 aircrew who saved Britain in the summer of 1940 included pilots from Poland, New Zealand, Canada, France, Czechoslovakia, Australia and elsewhere.*

WWII FACTS

CASUALTY FIGURES

15 August 1940 was the start of the Battle of Britain. The Luftwaffe lost 75 aircraft compared to 32 for the Royal Air Force Fighter Command, as shown on this document marked "Most Secret". For the next month, German losses continued to be high, and their factories were not producing as many new aircraft as the British.

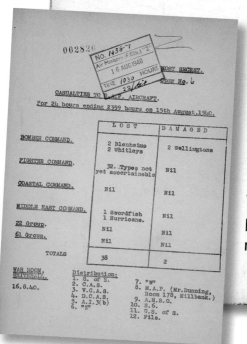

▲ *This report details how the British public felt about the war in August 1940. If people stopped supporting the war or the actions of the government this would weaken the war effort.*

13

BLITZ ON BRITAIN

After abandoning the invasion of Britain, Hitler and Luftwaffe chief Hermann Goering ordered huge fleets of bombers to bring the war into the heart of London and other cities. They hoped that these attacks would damage Britain's war economy and destroy the morale of its citizens. Thousands of tonnes of high explosives were dropped on London, especially the east end of the city, coastal towns such as Southampton, and industrial centres.

▲ From 7 September 1940, London was attacked by German bombers on 57 nights in a row.

Black outs

Air attacks had been expected from the start. The cities were blacked out so there were no lights to guide the bombers. In the poorer districts families queued to sleep in the public shelters as the wail of air raid sirens went on around them. Others slept in corrugated iron Anderson shelters. People living in London sought shelter in the nearest underground station.

In the final few months of 1940, 23,000 civilians were killed and more than 30,000 seriously injured by the bombs. For the most part, the attacks strengthened the British people's resolve to defeat Hitler, but there were also examples of terror, panic, and the fear that invasion was still likely at any time.

▶ This map shows how the German navigation signals made clear that hundreds of aircraft were heading for Coventry on 14 November 1940. Even if the British knew about the raid there was little they could do to stop it.

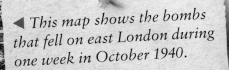

◄ This map shows the bombs that fell on east London during one week in October 1940.

◄ ▲ St Paul's Cathedral in London surrounded by the smoke of the bombs and fires, and the scene after the smoke had cleared.

SECRET WAR

Intelligence and information were just as important as military strength in World War II. Secret agents were used to gather information about the enemy, but secret services also had double agents who deliberately fed false information from one side to the other.

The Abwehr was the German intelligence service. Many members of the Abwehr, including its leader Admiral Canaris, were secret opponents of Hitler. Hitler's Nazi Party also had their own security organizations, the SD and the Gestapo, which spent much of their time spying on the Abwehr.

Allied intelligence services included Britain's MI5, which was responsible for dealing with threats to Britain, and MI6 or the Secret Intelligence Service, which ran networks of spies overseas. From 1942, the Office of Strategic Services (OSS) did a similar job for the United States.

Double agents

MI5 was particularly successful at managing double agents. After the war, MI5 discovered that they had caught almost all of the 115 German agents working in Britain, and some of them were actually working for the Allies.

WWII FACTS

AGENT ZIGZAG

Eddie Chapman was a bank robber before the war. He was in prison on the island of Jersey, near the French coast, when the Germans invaded. Chapman offered to work as a spy for the Abwehr. After parachuting into England with his forged ID card, Chapman turned himself in to MI5. Chapman was sent back into occupied Europe as a British agent. His deception was so good that the Nazis even awarded him a medal, believing agent Zigzag was really working for them.

▲ *Double agents knew the risks if they were caught. Johann Jebsen worked as a double agent for Britain. Shortly before D-Day he was captured, tortured and probably killed by the Nazis.*

"I want to know where your unit is stationed —so that I can bomb you and drop parachute troops to machine-gun you. This information I will get from you and your friends—please continue to give your friends military details. I shall hear." *Lieutenant-General Schultz* GERMAN INTELLIGENCE.

▲ This poster warns Allied troops not to share military details that could help the enemy.

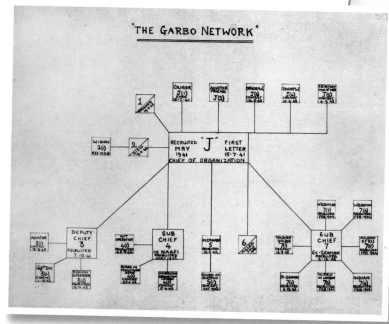

▲ This photo helped the public to identify German spies like the man on the left, who apparently wore worn clothing because of wartime shortages.

'THE GARBO NETWORK'

WWII FACTS

THE GARBO NETWORK

Spanish Juan Pujol-Garcia, codenamed Garbo, contacted German agents and offered to spy for them. He even convinced them that he was running a network of spies in Great Britain, when he was actually working for the British. Garbo's greatest achievement was to feed misinformation about the location of the D-Day landings. This helped ensure the success of the invasion and saved many lives.

CODEBREAKERS

In wartime, the element of surprise can be the key to victory. Knowing what the enemy will do next is almost priceless. Both sides knew the importance of keeping their communications secret, and breaking the complex codes used by the enemy was a major priority.

▲ *An Enigma machine, captured by the British.*

A German Enigma machine created coded messages and looked like a typewriter. An operator typed in a message and a system of wheels with letters on them would scramble it into a message that could only be read by someone who knew the settings of the code. Hundreds of mathematicians at Bletchley Park, Buckinghamshire, worked to keep up with the constantly changing codes. Alan Turing led a team to create an early computer, called the Bombe, which could decipher the code.

▲ *Alan Turing.*

Ultra secret

If the enemy ever discovered that their code had been deciphered, the advantage would be gone. High-level messages read in this way were codenamed Ultra and could only be viewed by the most senior and trusted people.

Hunting the U-boats

One of the greatest challenges for Bletchley Park was to crack coded messages sent to U-boat submarines that were attacking Allied ships. The Allies were able to capture several Enigma machines, which helped them to stay one step ahead of the German navy. However, successes like this could be short lived. For most of 1942, a new, more complex code had been developed by the enemy and could not be deciphered.

▲ *This document forms part of Turing's explanation of the mathematical theory behind the Enigma code.*

▲ During the war many versions of the Bombe machine were built. Several were kept at different locations in case one was destroyed by enemy attack.

CRACKING ENIGMA

Much of the work on cracking the Enigma code was done by Polish mathematicians before the war started. The Polish handed over their knowledge to British Intelligence just a few weeks before Poland was invaded.

▲ The Colossus electronic computer was built in 1943 to help with the unscrambling of German army codes.

OPERATION BARBAROSSA

In the early hours of 22 June 1941, Hitler took a huge gamble. He had invaded Yugoslavia and Greece in April. If he could invade the Soviet Union to seize oil for the German war machine, and food for the German people, Hitler would be invincible. Britain would have to make peace. The Nazis expected their plan would cause 30 million deaths from starvation.

▼ *German forces crossing the Soviet border in June 1941.*

Hitler's plan was a gamble because the Soviet Union could call on 14 million trained soldiers. However, these vast armies were unprepared for the invasion. After all, Soviet leader Stalin had signed a treaty with Hitler in 1939. The German forces quickly advanced deep into Soviet territory. The army was ordered to shoot all Communist Party members and Jews. The Soviet people destroyed cities and industry in the invaders' path so the German supplies would be stretched to the limit. But, by the beginning of October, German forces were close to the capital Moscow.

Siege of Leningrad

Leningrad (now called St Petersburg) was under siege for more than two years from September 1941. People starved or froze as all supplies had to come across a frozen lake. The people of Leningrad were reduced to eating crows or even carpenter's glue, scraped off the furniture they burned for heat. More people died in this one city than in the entire British and American war efforts.

▲ An officer of the Red Army urges his troops on against the invading forces.

WWII FACTS

UNLIKELY ALLIES

The war brought some unlikely allies together against a common enemy. Soviet leader Joseph Stalin stands alongside Adolf Hitler as one of history's cruellest leaders. His brutal dictatorship caused the deaths of many millions of his own people. However, without the Soviet Union's heroic struggle, Hitler may never have been defeated. In this poster, the British aristocrat Churchill and the communist dictator Stalin are shown as comrades.

The extreme cold of the winter, and desperate defence from the Soviet Union's Red Army stopped Hitler's advance in 1941. However, in 1942, the armies of Germany and her allies pushed south, hoping to capture the oil they had come for.

Comrades in Arms

JAPAN AND PEARL HARBOR

War in East Asia began several years before Hitler invaded Poland in 1939. Japan invaded the Chinese region of Manchuria in 1931 followed by an attack on the rest of China in 1937. In September 1940, Japan agreed a pact with Germany and Italy. Japanese forces then seized French and Dutch territories in Southeast Asia. As Japan flexed its muscles, protests from the United States and Britain grew louder.

Surprise attack

Japan's leaders believed that a sudden, dramatic defeat would convince the United States to stay out of the conflict. They tested this theory on 7 December 1941, with a surprise attack on the US naval base at Pearl Harbor, Hawaii. In a few minutes, Japanese aircraft destroyed or badly damaged eight American battleships and killed 2403 people. American President Franklin Roosevelt had tried to stay out of the war but the Japanese attack gave him no choice but to join the Allies.

▶ By the end of 1941, Britain had a new ally but also a new enemy in Japan.

Great Britain will pursue the **WAR AGAINST JAPAN** to the very end.
WINSTON CHURCHILL

The British Empire still included many colonies in Asia, but they were now in grave danger from Japanese attack. In the weeks after Pearl Harbor, Japanese forces marched across Southeast Asia. Japanese tanks rolled into Singapore in February 1942. Burma was attacked so the Japanese could cut off supplies to China. The Japanese invasion of Asia and the islands of the Pacific moved so fast that Australia and New Zealand feared that they would be next. American forces were being readied for war, but it could all be too late.

▼ The battleship USS Arizona burns after being hit during the Japanese attack on Pearl Harbor.

▲ Japan's troops invading a Pacific island in 1942.

WWII FACTS

TIPPING THE BALANCE

This cartoon was produced by the British Ministry of Information. America's entry into the war meant a big shift in power, and a boost to morale in Britain. Could Hitler land a punch on the mighty USA, and its President Franklin Roosevelt?

▲ President Roosevelt built a close relationship with Winston Churchill.

NORTH AFRICA AND THE MEDITERRANEAN

When Italy joined the war as an ally of Germany in June 1940, the conflict spread to another continent as Italian troops attacked the British in North Africa. The Italians were forced to retreat as British forces captured the Libyan city of Tobruk in January 1941. In response, Hitler sent one of his best generals to North Africa – Erwin Rommel, known as the 'Desert Fox'.

▲ *General Bernard Montgomery masterminded almost the first Allied victory of the war at El Alamein.*

Rommel's campaign of fast-moving tank warfare was well suited to the heat and dust of the desert. Despite having a larger force and better supply lines, British troops were regularly outsmarted by Rommel. Finally, in late 1942, the new Allied commander, General Bernard Montgomery, forced Rommel to fight in a tight space surrounded by ridges and minefields. The German tanks had little room to move and the Allies finally won a victory at the Battle of El Alamein.

Operation Torch

To the west, British and American troops landed on the coasts of Morocco in November 1942. Operation Torch enabled the Allies to encircle Rommel as he retreated. The war in North Africa ended in May 1943 with the capture of 250,000 troops from Germany and her allies, called the Axis powers.

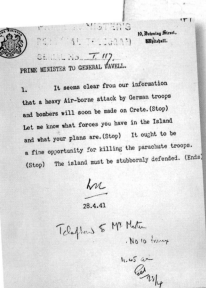

WWII FACTS

ADVANCE WARNING

This top secret message from Winston Churchill to General Wavell, his commander-in-chief in North Africa, was sent almost a month before German paratroopers invaded Crete. Cracking the German codes warned the Allies about the invasion. The Germans suffered heavy losses but were eventually able to seize the island.

Malta

The island of Malta was vital for both sides as a base for naval and air control of the Mediterranean Sea, and to disrupt supplies going to North Africa. The British-controlled island was besieged by Axis aircraft and naval power from 1940 until 1942, with defenders and ordinary people facing shortages of food and supplies. The Allies lost numerous ships trying to supply and defend Malta before the Allied victory in North Africa ended the siege.

▲ In desert warfare, there were no obstacles to hide behind. The armies used other methods such as this dummy artillery gun to fool the enemy.

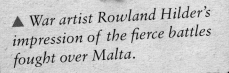

▲ War artist Rowland Hilder's impression of the fierce battles fought over Malta.

▲ British and American troops land on the coast of Morocco during Operation Torch.

OCCUPATION AND RESISTANCE

As Allied and Axis forces battled in North Africa and the Soviet Union, much of Europe was under Nazi control. Lands on the border of Germany had become part of the German "fatherland", ruled directly from Berlin. The central area of Poland was named the General Government under Nazi rule. Nazi troops were occupying Denmark, Norway, the Netherlands, Belgium and much of France. In countries such as Italy, Hungary, Croatia and southern France, the governments were Hitler's allies or largely under his control.

Living under Nazi rule

People living in occupied Europe found life very tough, even if they were not part of groups such as Jews and Roma who were singled out for persecution. Everyone lived in constant fear that they would attract the attention of the feared SS, the Nazis' all-powerful state police who used torture and murder to achieve their aims. Food was scarce as Germany took a proportion of crops to feed its people and armies.

Resisting the invaders

Some people chose to work with the invaders, such as the Ukrainians who served as guards in the terrible concentration camps. Others bravely

WWII FACTS

SABOTAGE SECRETS

German agents carried some ingenious sabotage devices, such as this exploding chocolate bar. Although these were never used in Britain, several were seized in Turkey.

THE BOMB IS MADE OF STEEL WITH A THIN COVERING OF REAL CHOCOLATE. WHEN THE PIECE OF CHOCOLATE AT THE END IS BROKEN OFF THE CANVAS SHOWN IS PULLED, AND AFTER A DELAY OF SEVEN SECONDS THE BOMB EXPLODES.

CANVAS

STEEL ENDS

▼ *This map shows the location of resistance groups in Italy after 1943.*

▲ *A convoy of Nazi officials drives into Amsterdam, the capital of the Netherlands, in 1940.*

chose to risk their lives in resisting the Nazis. In western countries such as France, the resistance movements used sabotage to make life difficult for German forces. In Yugoslavia and Greece, partisans hid in the mountains and attacked German forces when they could.

The risks were huge, not just for the fighters who faced execution if they were caught, but also for ordinary people. The killing of a single Nazi officer could be punished with mass murder and destruction of whole villages, as happened in the Czech village of Lidice.

▼ *This British poster praises the work of the French Resistance, who would play an important role in the Allied invasion of France on D-Day.*

Salut à la Résistance
-et en avant!

Behind enemy lines

The resistance movements in Nazi-occupied Europe were supported by the Special Operations Executive (SOE). Churchill set up the SOE to "set Europe ablaze". Agents were trained to work in secret behind enemy lines, helping the resistance and launching sabotage attacks. This secret unit began in 1940 based in two London flats but by 1945 13,000 people were working for the SOE.

The SOE's agents were trained in safe houses across Britain. They learned unarmed combat and how to survive without support after they parachuted into Nazi Europe. Scientists and camouflage experts worked on special equipment to help them survive and to damage the enemy, including exploding rats and tree trunk mould that could be used to hide radio equipment.

▶ *This map shows arms deliveries to the French Resistance by SOE agents.*

RATS, EXPLOSIVE.

PRIMER

P.E.

PENCIL TIME FUSE

▲ *The explosive rat was designed to detonate inside enemy boilers. It would be left on a pile of coal and when it was added to a coal fire, the seemingly ordinary dead rat would explode.*

Sabotage successes

The SOE's greatest successes included blowing up a power station in France that stopped work on a German U-boat base. In 1945, the SOE destroyed a plant in Norway that was a vital part of Nazi plans to create an atomic bomb.

Other parts of British Intelligence were suspicious of the SOE. Some agents were believed to be double agents working for Germany. For example, the SOE radio sets in the Netherlands were discovered and used by the Germans to lure British agents into danger. Many agents were captured as they parachuted directly into the hands of the enemy.

▲ *SOE agents needed expertly forged documents from passports to luggage labels so they could avoid capture. SOE agents even created this false passport for Adolf Hitler as a joke to show off their skills.*

WWII FACTS

SPECIAL AGENT FIFI

The SOE had to be sure that their agents would not spill their secrets. The lives of other agents and resistance fighters could be at stake. 'Fifi' was a renowned agent who was used to befriend trainees. 'Fifi' was extremely beautiful and she would pretend to be a French journalist offering to help with the trainee's mission. If the student gave away too much information, they failed the test. Fifi's true identity remained a secret until 2014. Her real name was Marie Christine Chilver.

▼ *This ordinary looking suitcase could be used to carry secret documents. The case had to be opened in a special way. If it was opened normally, the case would explode and catch fire.*

THE WAR AT SEA

From the very start of the war, the Atlantic Ocean was a key battlefield. Britain relied on supplies of food and other materials coming from North America. Merchant ships travelled to Britain in convoys protected by warships, but they were still vulnerable to attack by German U-boats.

▲ Saint Nazaire in France was one of the main U-boat bases. This aerial photo shows the reinforced concrete bunker that housed Germany's secret weapon. Saint Nazaire's port was badly damaged by a daring Allied commando raid in March 1942.

WWII FACTS

RADAR

New technology had a vital part to play in defeating the U-boats. Radar detects unseen objects by sending out a blast of radio waves and seeing if they bounce back off an object, such as an aircraft or ship. Allied forces developed radar that could be carried by ships and aircraft. A German U-boat on the surface could be attacked and destroyed before its crew knew they had been detected.

During 1941 and 1942, German U-boats had great success against Allied shipping. Although aircraft could target submarines close to Europe and North America, there was an area in the mid-Atlantic where U-boats could hunt in safety. By 1943, the Allies were able to cover this gap. Growing German U-boat losses meant that convoys and United States troops for the invasion of Europe were able to move more freely.

Battles of the Pacific

Naval power was also crucial in the United States' battle against Japan. Fortunately, American aircraft carriers were undamaged by the attack on Pearl Harbour. These new weapons were vital in United States' victories at the Battles of the Coral Sea and Midway in 1942.

PLATE 12.

MERCHANT SHIPS SUNK BY U-BOAT IN THE ATLANTIC

WWII FACTS

COUNTING THE COST

These maps show the number of merchant ships sunk in the Battle of the Atlantic. They show that the German U-boats had most success in 1941 and 1942. In total, more than 2800 merchant ships were sunk and 40,000 sailors killed in the Battle of the Atlantic. Germany lost 781 U-boats. Being a submariner was possibly the most dangerous job in wartime as two-thirds of all U-boat crews were killed.

▲ *U-boat U-570 surrenders to a British warship. Captured submarines could contain valuable equipment and information for cracking enemy codes.*

◀ *Aircraft being prepared for launch from the deck of USS Enterprise during the Battle of Midway.*

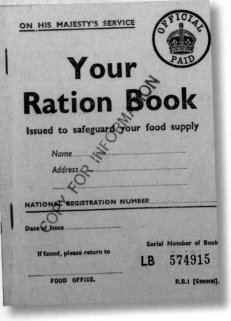

▲ Shoppers became used to queuing in shops to get their ration books stamped.

HOME FRONTS

World War II was a 'total war', involving all the people, industry and resources of the warring countries. More civilians died in the conflict than soldiers on the battlefield. Even those people who were not caught up in the fighting or occupied by an invading army faced the regular danger of air attack. Every man, woman and child experienced changes to their lives, from the food they ate to the jobs they did.

Rationing

Essential foods such as sugar, meat and eggs were rationed in Britain from the beginning of 1940. German U-boat attacks in the Atlantic stopped many foods reaching the country. Rationing was designed to make sure that there was enough food for everyone. Other goods rationed included petrol, clothes and soap. Rationing of butter and margarine was introduced in Germany before the war even started. For most of the war, Germans did not go hungry, as the German government took food from the lands occupied by their troops.

MAKE-DO AND MEND *says Mrs. Sew-and-Sew*

▲ Government posters urged people to mend their clothes rather than buy new ones.

War economy

In Britain and the United States, Government poster campaigns encouraged people to do whatever they could to support the war effort. 'Dig for Victory' was one slogan that called for every available piece of land to be used to grow food. In the United States, there was a great drive to collect and recycle metal so it could be used for war equipment. Many factories that had previously produced everyday goods switched to producing aircraft or other supplies for the war effort.

Skin the cod, cut it into pieces about 3 inches long. Place in layers in a greased casserole, sprinkling each layer with paprika. Add the mill... the lid on the casserole and cook in a moderate oven for 30 minutes. ...in the fish, keeping the liquid and making it up to ½ pint with milk or water. Keep the fish hot in the casserole while making the sauce. Blend the dry ingredients with a little of the fish liquid and made mustard. Boil the rest of the liquid and, when boiling, add it to the blended ingredients. Return to the pan and stir until it boils. Boil gently for 5 minutes. Stir in the vinegar and pour the sauce over the fish. Serve hot.

CHEESE SAUSAGE ROLLS

1 oz. fat
4 oz. flour
Pinch of salt

2 oz. grated cheese
Water to mix
½ lb. sausagemeat

Rub the fat into the flour and salt. Add the grated cheese and mix to a stiff dough with water. Roll out and cut into 8 oblongs, about 3" x 4". Roll the sausagemeat into 8 sausages, about 2½" long, and form into sausage rolls with the pastry. Bake in a hot oven for 25-30 minutes.

N.B. The fat may be omitted if the amount of cheese is increased from 2-4 ozs.

HOT POTATO SALAD

1½ lb. potatoes, sliced
1 small onion or leek, sliced
2-4 oz. bacon, diced
3 tablespoons vinegar
½ level teaspoon mustard

1 level tablespoon sugar
¼ pint water
Salt and pepper
2 tablespoons chopped parsley

Place all the ingredients, except parsley, in a pan and simmer until the potatoes are tender. Add the chopped parsley and serve.

RHUBARB JELLY

½ pint of water
½ lb. prepared rhubarb
2 tablespoons sugar

1 tablespoon syrup
1½ tablespoons powdered gelatine
Cochineal colouring if necessary

Bring the water and the rhubarb to the boil. Boil gently for 10 minutes with the syrup and the sugar. Mix the gelatine with a little cold water. Remove the pan from the heat, and pour the hot liquid on to the gelatine. Stir until dissolved. Add cochineal if required. Turn into moulds and allow to set.

RHUBARB CRUMBLE

1 lb. rhubarb
2 tablespoons syrup
1½ oz. fat

4 oz. plain flour
Pinch of salt
3 tablespoons sugar

Wipe rhubarb and cut into small pieces. Simmer with the syrup until cooked and place at the bottom ... ...f... the flour salt and sugar until like fine ... stewed fruit. Bake in a moderat...

Issued by the Ministry of Food

▼ A truck crosses a frozen lake delivering essential supplies to the besieged Soviet city of Leningrad.

▲ This calendar gave families ideas on how to cook nutritious meals with the rations they were allowed.

WWII FACTS

FAMINE IN INDIA

Food supplies were protected in Britain through strict rationing, but the story was very different in British-controlled India. Japan's invasion of Burma reduced supplies of rice to India, causing shortages and price rises. The government failed to act and the result was a terrible famine in 1942 that claimed more than 1.5 million lives.

The need is 'GROWING'...

DIG FOR VICTORY STILL

▲ The British people were urged to grow more food as imports were hit by the war.

WOMEN AT WAR

In the total war that erupted around the world, women were just as much a target for the bombing raids and other attacks as anybody else. They also played vital roles in winning the war. In the Soviet Union, women fought as fighter pilots, snipers and machine gunners. The British government introduced conscription for single women between the ages of 20 and 30 in December 1941. These conscripts did not fight on the frontline but worked to support the armed forces and did essential war work.

More than 250,000 women joined military organizations such as the Army Territorial Service (ATS) or the Women's Royal Naval Service (WRNS). As well as doing support duties such as cooking and administrative work, members of these services worked as mechanics, radar operators, drivers and delivery operators. In the United States, around 200,000 women joined the Army and Navy auxiliary services.

Women at work

Female workers took on many important jobs from men who were serving in the armed forces. One-third of British factory workers were women, making the aircraft, tanks and ships that would enable the Allies to win the war.

▼ *It was essential for the railways to be kept running during the war.*

WWII FACTS

WOMEN'S LAND ARMY

The Women's Land Army was set up in 1939 to help out on the farms that were so essential for the nation's food supply. By 1943, there were 80,000 'land girls'. Many land girls came from cities such as London and had very little training. They worked hard, in all weathers, and were not well paid.

'We could do with thousands more like you..'

JOIN THE WOMEN'S LAND ARMY

▲ These members of the ATS are plotting the positions of ships. This had to be done by hand as there were no computer or video screens at the time.

◀ This poster makes women working in factories appear as war heroes.

WOMEN OF BRITAIN

COME INTO THE FACTORIES

ASK AT ANY EMPLOYMENT EXCHANGE FOR ADVICE AND FULL DETAILS

CHILDREN'S LIVES IN WARTIME

All children's lives changed during wartime. For some, the war meant separation from parents who were fighting overseas. Others were forced to leave their homes by enemy bombing raids. In Britain, hundreds of thousands of children were evacuated from the cities to the safety of the countryside. Millions of children across the world found their own lives in danger, or lost loved ones.

▲ *This poster appealed to families outside the cities to take in evacuees. It points out that the children's parents were often in the armed forces or other war work.*

Evacuation

More than 1.5 million children and adults were evacuated from British cities when war broke out, although they often returned home when the promised air raids did not happen. Many came from the poorest areas of the cities and brought nothing with them but the clothes they were wearing. Other families made their own decision to go and stay with relatives in the country. Thousands of families chose not to evacuate their children, but quickly changed their minds when Britain was threatened by invasion and the Blitz in 1940.

WWII FACTS

KINDERTRANSPORT

Many Jewish families were forced out of Germany by Nazi persecution during the 1930s. The Kindertransport was a British operation to rescue Jewish children from territories occupied by the Nazis. Nearly 10,000 children were rescued between 1938 and the outbreak of war in 1939. This document includes some of their names. The Kindertransport saved these children's lives, but many never saw their families again.

Children helped in the war effort too, especially the millions of young people who were members of youth groups such as the Boy Scouts and Girl Guides. Teenagers who stayed in the cities helped out as messengers and fire-watchers during the Blitz.

Children under attack

Most children in Germany were not evacuated during the war, and thousands were killed when the Allies bombed German cities. This was also the case when the United States bombed Japanese cities. Millions of families were made homeless by the fighting.

▲ Young people were happy to make their own contribution to the war effort. These children are helping to 'dig for victory' and grow food.

THE PROPAGANDA WAR

Adolf Hitler knew the importance of propaganda. When he became leader of Germany in 1933, he set up the Ministry of Public Enlightenment and Propaganda directed by Josef Goebbels. Its job was to promote the Nazi message of German strength and to spread hatred of the Nazis' enemies. The Nazis also made sure to ban all art, music, books or newspapers that did not promote their own view of the world.

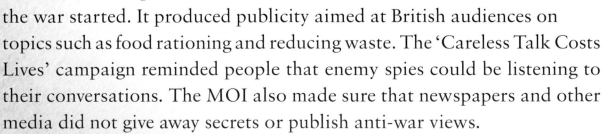

▶ Celebrating victories and the bravery of Allied forces helped to convince ordinary people that victory would come.

Propaganda is any information or media that deliberately promotes only one point of view, usually that of a government. When war broke out, all governments used propaganda to raise the morale of their own people and attack the enemy.

British propaganda

The British Ministry of Information (MOI) had been planned even before the war started. It produced publicity aimed at British audiences on topics such as food rationing and reducing waste. The 'Careless Talk Costs Lives' campaign reminded people that enemy spies could be listening to their conversations. The MOI also made sure that newspapers and other media did not give away secrets or publish anti-war views.

Political warfare

Britain set up the Political Warfare Executive in 1941, which created materials that would damage enemy morale. They produced radio broadcasts in German to undermine Nazi propaganda messages. Leaflets were dropped behind enemy lines in an attempt to convince Germans to turn against their leaders.

German air raids and fear of invasion ensured that support for the war never wavered on the Allied side. Josef Goebbels wrote in his diary that, as the war wore on and there were more German defeats, Germans started to pay more attention to Allied leaflets and radio broadcasts.

▲ Letters to and from soldiers serving overseas were read and censored to make sure they contained no information that could help the enemy.

▼ This Allied propaganda poster was produced in Cairo, as part of the campaign in North Africa.

يوم الشعوب المتحدة

WWII FACTS

LORD HAW HAW

American-born William Joyce, known as Lord Haw Haw, broadcast Nazi propaganda from Germany to Britain. Living in Britain before the war, he had been a committed supporter of Nazi ideas. He was executed for treason after the war. Joyce's broadcasts supposedly contained details of which towns would be bombed by the Germans. Often these were just rumours intended to cause panic.

AXIS POWERS IN RETREAT

The Allies first real significant victory came in the North African heat in late 1942. At the same time, the Soviet Union began to turn the tide. The Soviet fight back began in the icy depths of the Russian winter at Stalingrad.

For the Soviet Union, Stalingrad was a battle of survival. If German forces could triumph here, they could capture the valuable oil fields and encircle Moscow. The battle-scarred Red Army fought for every building in the city, finally managing to put a stop to the German advance in November 1942. They encircled the attackers and on 1 February 1943, German commander General Paulus surrendered.

WWII FACTS

KURSK

The Battle of Kursk in the Soviet Union, in July 1943 was the largest land battle in history. Soviet and German forces included three million men, 13,000 tanks and 12,000 aircraft. In 12 days of fighting, the Soviet Union lost more than 300,000 men compared to German losses of 55,000. But the Soviet Union's Red Army could afford to take the losses, while Germany's resources were getting stretched.

▲ *US troops crossing a temporary bridge in Italy as they try to force back Axis forces during 1944.*

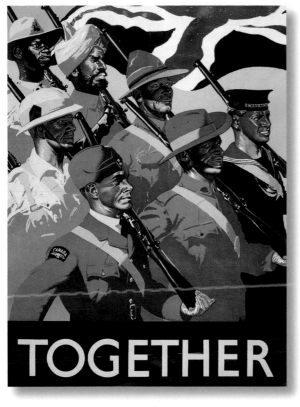

In 1940 Britain had been almost alone, but by 1943 the Axis Powers were heavily outnumbered by Allied forces.

Italian invasion

On 10 July 1943, Allied forces from North Africa invaded the Italian island of Sicily. By 17 August, German and Italian troops had been forced from the island. Allied forces landed on mainland Italy in September. Italy changed sides but the Allied campaign was not over, as their troops battled their way north against German forces.

In November, Roosevelt, Stalin and Churchill met at the Tehran conference. With Germany on the defensive at last, Churchill reluctantly agreed to an invasion of France in 1944.

WWII FACTS

OPERATION MINCEMEAT

In 1943, the body of a British naval officer, William Martin, was found floating off the coast of Spain. He was carrying a top-secret document about Allied plans for an invasion of Greece. This information reached Nazi commanders via their spies in neutral Spain. The Nazis moved 90,000 troops to prepare for the invasion. But William Martin was actually a homeless man called Glyndwr Michael, who had died in London, and the real invasion was planned for Sicily. Operation Mincemeat was a trick dreamed up by British Intelligence to fool the enemy. The officer in charge of the operation wrote to Churchill saying, "Mincemeat swallowed rod, line and sinker."

GERMANY UNDER ATTACK

While Germany's armies were advancing across Europe, their bombing raids destroyed cities such as Coventry in Britain and Rotterdam in the Netherlands. However, after 1941, German cities were flattened by Allied 'area bombing', which was designed to hit the morale of the German people.

▲ *Raids could include up to 1000 aircraft like this Lancaster bomber.*

Air Marshal Arthur 'Bomber' Harris was in charge of RAF Bomber Command. Harris believed that bombing cities would win the war, even though Germany's leaders were much more worried about attacks on their factories and oil supplies. Huge bombing raids were launched against cities such as Hamburg and Berlin. British bombers usually attacked at night and the Americans attacked in daylight, supported by fighter aircraft.

◄ *Arthur 'Bomber' Harris believed that the bombing of German cities would bring the war to an end more quickly.*

WWII FACTS

DAMBUSTERS

Dr Barnes Wallis designed a special bouncing bomb that he believed could destroy German dams if it was released from the right height at the right distance from the dam. His plans are shown here. Wing Commander Guy Gibson and the pilots of RAF 617 Squadron were tasked with the daring Dambusters raid of 16 May 1943. The raid destroyed four dams and flooded Germany's industrial heartland.

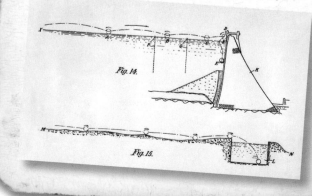

Justifying area bombing

Many people have questioned whether the death and destruction caused by these raids did help to win the war. After the destruction of Dresden in Germany just a few weeks from the end of the war, Churchill himself wrote, "I feel the need for more precise concentration on military objectives…rather than on mere acts of terror and wanton destruction, however impressive".

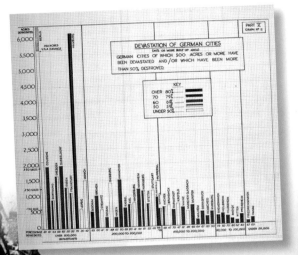

▲ This chart showed which German cities had been bombed and how much damage the raids had done.

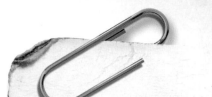

WWII FACTS

THE HUMAN COST

In 1943, less than one in five bomber crews survived for a full tour of duty of 30 bombing missions. More than 160,000 Allied airmen lost their lives in the war. More than 500,000 German men, women and children perished in the raids.

This chart was produced to show what proportion of Allied bombing raids actually hit their 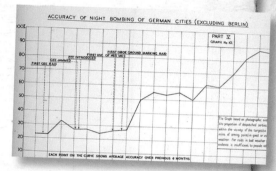 targets. Developments in radar and tracking technology made the raids more accurate. The low success rate of early bombing raids led to the attacks being targeted at whole cities rather than specific industrial and military targets.

◀ This photo shows the destruction caused by an attack on the city of Hamburg in 1943.

OPERATION OVERLORD

The first plan for Operation Overlord, the Allied invasion of France, was prepared in summer 1943. Working in utmost secrecy, Britain, the United States and the other Allies determined that the massive invasion force would land on the beaches of Normandy. If the invasion was to be successful, the Allies would have to plan every last detail, keeping their plans secret from the enemy. They would also need support from the resistance fighters within France.

WWII FACTS

OPERATION TITANIC

The night before D-Day, hundreds of dummy parachutists were dropped at various points in Normandy to confuse the defenders. This was known as 'Operation Titanic'. These cloth dummies were designed to catch fire on landing so it looked as if real paratroopers had burned their parachutes to stop them being found.

Decoy and deception

If the Germans had known where the invasion would take place, they could have concentrated their forces in one place but they could not be certain where or when the attack would come. Fake camps were built in south east England to convince them that the attack would be across the narrowest point of the English Channel, and in Scotland to pretend that Norway was the target. Double agent Garbo also fed false information to the enemy.

▶ *German coded messages told the Allies if their deception had worked and what the enemy knew about the invasion. This report from May 1944 confirms that the invasion force was almost ready but the Germans did not know when the invasion would come.*

◄ Part of the massive invasion force that landed in Normandy during Operation Overlord.

▲ The French city of Caen was devastated as the Allies fought their way from the Normandy coast.

Planning for success

The Normandy landings were planned meticulously. The Allies had even secretly collected samples of sand from the beaches to see whether the sand would bear the weight of their tanks. Even with these preparations in place, the German defences would still be formidable.

The D-Day landings were successful. US troops landing on Omaha Beach had to face the fiercest fighting and suffered around 3000 casualties. That was just the first step and it was several weeks before the Allies could battle their way out of Normandy. German counter-attacks eventually failed and, on 24 August 1944, Paris was liberated after four years of German occupation.

WWII FACTS

AIRBORNE INVASION

Thousands of Allied paratroopers were dropped into northern France a few hours before the seaborne invasion. Strong winds and anti-aircraft fire forced many of them off course, confusing the enemy about their real objectives.

TERROR AND PERSECUTION

Nazi rule in Germany and elsewhere had been built on hate and fear. This was especially true in Eastern Europe, where Hitler wanted to create extra 'living space' for the German people. He believed that terrorizing, persecuting and murdering the people who he conquered would help him to achieve this.

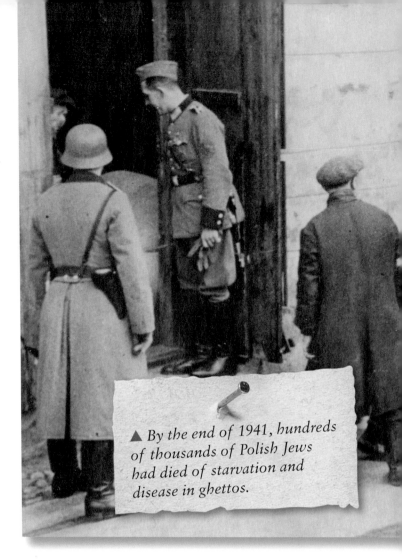

▲ By the end of 1941, hundreds of thousands of Polish Jews had died of starvation and disease in ghettos.

While the people of Western Europe had to suffer many injuries and crimes at the hands of the Nazis, the worst treatment was reserved for the people seen as inferior in the terrible Nazi worldview. These included Slavs from Eastern Europe, Roma people and, most of all, Jews.

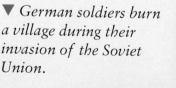

▼ German soldiers burn a village during their invasion of the Soviet Union.

From 1933 onwards, the Nazis built a network of concentration camps to imprison their political enemies. The camp system grew dramatically after the invasion of Poland in 1939. The Germans also set up labour camps where non-Germans were forced to work for the German war effort.

Ghettos

Some Jews and victims of race hatred were sent to these camps, while Jews from across occupied Europe were crammed into ghettos. These were areas of cities, often

▲ In Eastern Europe, both sides ignored international rules on the treatment of prisoners of war. Soviet prisoners were allowed to die of starvation and disease, and German prisoners captured by Stalin's forces were not treated any better.

enclosed by barbed wire, where Jews were forced to live with very little food, sanitation or medical supplies. There were around 1000 such ghettos in Europe.

The ghettos were a way to separate Jews from the rest of the population while the Nazis decided their fate.

WWII FACTS

JAPANESE RULE

Japanese occupation of Southeast Asia could be just as brutal as the Nazi regime in Europe. In Singapore, the Chinese community was singled out for terrible treatment, including the murder of thousands of people. Around five million people died as a result of Japanese rule in Asia.

◀ The Star of David on this concentration camp uniform shows that it was worn by a prisoner whose only crime was to be Jewish.

THE NAZIS' 'FINAL SOLUTION'

In July 1941, Reinhard Heydrich, a senior officer in the SS, was ordered to devise a "final solution to the Jewish question". His plan, which was approved at a conference in January 1942, was nothing less than the murder of 11 million Jews across Europe.

Jews across Europe were transported from their home countries to camps in Poland and Eastern Europe. Those who were physically strong would be put to work. Others would be murdered on an industrial scale. More than one million people were sent to the largest death camp at Auschwitz. Further east, Jewish ghettos were destroyed and the inhabitants killed. In total, around six million Jews died in the Holocaust.

▼ *Allied codebreakers started picking up reports of widespread killing of Jews shortly after the invasion of the Soviet Union in 1941. This document from 1942 warns about the Nazi plans to murder all Jews in occupied Europe.*

▼ *Survivors of Auschwitz concentration camp when it was finally liberated in January 1945.*

[CYPHER].

FROM BERNE TO FOREIGN OFFICE.

Mr. Norton.   D. 4.48 p.m. August 10th, 1942.
No. 2851.   R. 6.25 p.m. August 10th, 1942.
August 10th, 1942.

                        yyyyyy
      Following from His Majesty's Consul General at Geneva No. 174 (Begins).

      Following for Mr. S.S. Silverman M.P., Chairman of British Section, World Jewish Congress London from Mr. Gerhart Riegner Secretary of World Jewish Congress, Geneva.

      [Begins].

      Received alarming report stating that, in the Fuehrer's Headquarters, a plan has been discussed, and is under consideration according to which all Jews in countries occupied or controlled by Germany numbering 3½ to 4 millions should, after deportation and concentration in the East, be at one blow exterminated, in order to resolve, once and for all the Jewish question in Europe. Action is reported to be planned for the autumn. Ways of execution are still being discussed including the use of prussic acid. We transmit this information with all the necessary reservation, as exactitude cannot be confirmed by us. Our informant is reported to have close connexions with the highest German authorities, and his reports are generally reliable. Please inform and consult New York. (Ends].

Who knew about the Holocaust?

While the orders for the Holocaust came from the top of the Nazi Party and were kept as secret as possible, thousands of people were involved in the administration of this gigantic crime. Many of the brutal camp guards were not German but came from the occupied countries of Eastern Europe. The Nazis' victims were transported across Europe tightly packed in windowless trains. The officials who organized these forced journeys, or ran the factories employing Jewish slave labour, knew something of what was going on. While some people risked their own lives to protect Jews, many who knew the truth remained silent.

WWII FACTS

WHAT DID THE ALLIES KNOW?

This report from 1942 shows that the Allies had some knowledge of what was happening. Around four million Jews were executed in that year. At that time, Nazi power was at its height. The full horrors of camps such as Auschwitz and Belsen were not discovered until they were found in 1945, but could the Allies have done more to stop the Holocaust?

MOST SECRET

40/42. 2.

10. Reports on deaths in German prison camps during August reveal the following figures:-

NIEDERHAGEN: 21; AUSCHWITZ: 6829 men, 1525 women; FLOSSENBURG: 88; BUCHENWALD: 74. (1/9).

A message of 4/9, in reply to a request for 1000 prisoners for building the DANUBE railway, states that AUSCHWITZ cannot provide them until the "ban" (Lagersperre) on the AUSCHWITZ camp has been lifted. It appears that although typhus is still rife at AUSCHWITZ, new arrivals continue to come in.

11. As from 1/9/42, "natural deaths" among prisoners in Concentration Camps are to be reported apparently only in writing (durch Formblatt).

HITLER'S DOWNFALL

By the close of 1944, the end of the war was in sight. Both Germany and Japan were exhausted and surrounded by their enemies. But their leaders were determined to fight on until their inevitable defeat. The Nazi leaders knew that their crimes, and the thirst for revenge of the Soviet Union, meant that they could never make peace.

In October 1944, the armies that had invaded France reached the River Rhine, in western Germany. Hitler's forces launched one last counter-attack into Belgium, but this soon fizzled out. In the East, the Soviet Union's Red Army marched on towards Berlin. Germans and others fled ahead of the Soviet advance. They were desperate to reach the land controlled by the United States and British forces, who would treat the defeated Germans better than Stalin's vengeful army.

The two Allied armies met each other on 24 April, but the fighting continued in many areas including Hitler's capital Berlin. By the end of April, the Soviet army was fighting its way into Berlin and Hitler took his own life in his underground bunker in the city on 30 April.

▼ *The war left millions without homes or families, like this boy in the ruins of Warsaw, Poland.*

Victory in Europe

The final German surrender was agreed on 8 May 1945 and this was celebrated as Victory in Europe Day, or VE Day. There was excitement and relief in cities such as London and Paris. Hitler had promised to make Germany great again, but left behind a shattered country. Millions of Germans became refugees in their own country. Germans also had to face the horror of the death camps and the crimes that had been committed in their name.

▼ *German troops taken prisoner at Aachen on the German border in October 1944.*

▶ *This surrender of German forces was signed on 8 May 1945, ending the war in Europe.*

6. This Act is drawn up in the English, Russian and German languages. The English and Russian are the only authentic texts.

▼ *In 1944, Hitler unleashed a new menace on Britain. The V-1 and V-2 flying bombs were packed with enough explosive to destroy a whole street of houses. This public bomb shelter was destroyed by a V-1 or 'doodlebug' on 4 August 1944.*

WAR AND PEACE IN THE PACIFIC

Even after Hitler was defeated in Europe, Japan refused to surrender. The Pacific conflict was very different from the battles in Europe. Japanese forces were established in Southeast Asia and controlled many scattered islands of the Pacific. To get within striking distance of Japan, American forces had to capture these islands. One thing that the Japanese forces shared with the Nazis was their appalling treatment of their prisoners and the people who lived under their rule.

▲ *High school girls wave as a kamikaze pilot sets off on his final journey.*

Island assaults

Japanese soldiers fought fiercely to defend their island fortresses. Of the 30,000 men defending the island of Saipan, almost none survived the American assault as they refused to surrender. In 1944, the Americans got closer to Japan with the capture of the Marianas Islands and then the Philippines.

The might of American industry enabled them to build far more ships and aircraft than their enemy. By the end of 1944, American aircraft were close enough to launch bombing raids on Japanese cities. In February 1945, they captured the southern Japanese island of Iwo Jima. Japan's response grew even more desperate, as kamikaze pilots crashed their explosives-laden planes into American ships, killing many Americans and sacrificing their own lives.

▲ *By the time Churchill, Roosevelt and Stalin met at Yalta in February 1945 it was clear that the United States and the Soviet Union would dominate the world after the war.*

The final act

The United States then had to make a decision about whether to use a new and terrible weapon. Many thousands of American soldiers would be killed in invading Japan, and the war would last longer. President Harry Truman, who had taken office after the death of President Roosevelt, authorized the use of the first atomic bomb, developed over many years, on the city of Hiroshima.

Hiroshima was destroyed in a blinding flash of light and heat on 6 August 1945, killing 80,000 people. Another bomb was dropped on Nagasaki three days later, before Japan surrendered on 15 August. The most destructive, hate-filled conflict in history was finally over.

◄ *The atomic bomb explosion destroyed around half of the city of Nagasaki and claimed 30,000 lives.*

◄ *The bomb that exploded over Nagasaki had an explosive power equivalent to around 20,000 tonnes of TNT.*

Thirteen Japanese flying-boats were smashed in a heavy Royal Air Force raid on the harbour of Port Blair in the Andaman Islands.

SMASH JAPANESE AGGRESSION !

◄ *A British poster rallies support for the war against Japan. British, Indian and African troops battled the Japanese in the jungles of Burma until 1945.*

WWII FACTS

NO SURRENDER

One Japanese soldier continued the war for almost 30 years after the Japanese surrender. Lieutenant Hiroo Onoda carried on fighting on a remote Philippine island until March 1974. He refused to surrender until he received official orders from Japan.

WORLD WAR TO COLD WAR

As victory in World War II edged closer, it became clear that the post-war world would be very different. Two countries had emerged as global powers – the capitalist United States and the communist Soviet Union. Although these superpowers had fought together against Hitler, their political ideas were very different.

Cold War

Germany was divided between the area controlled by the Soviet Union, which became East Germany, and West Germany controlled by the United States and Britain. In East Germany, Stalin imposed a communist government, as he did in much of Soviet-controlled Eastern Europe. Western countries such as France might have been taken over by communists if the United States had not provided money for rebuilding. Under the Marshall Plan of 1947, the United States gave $17 billion to the devastated countries of Europe.

▲ *Allied leaders met several times to decide the shape of the post-war world. This note is from a meeting between Churchill and Stalin. The tick of agreement was made by the Soviet leader.*

▶ In 1961, *the communist authorities in East Berlin built a huge wall to stop people moving to the western part of the city. Here, US President Kennedy visits this symbol of the Cold War in 1963.*

The two superpowers, both with nuclear weapons after 1949, opposed each other in an uneasy mixture of peace and war until 1989, called the Cold War. The two parts of Germany were reunified in 1990.

While Britain had stood alone against the Nazis, the country was greatly weakened by the sacrifice of winning the war. In the Cold-War world, Britain's influence declined and most of the lands that had been part of its empire gained independence.

▼ *Surviving Nazi leaders on trial in 1945.*

WWII FACTS

NAZIS ON TRIAL

From November 1945, leading Nazis were put on trial for their role in the regime's crimes, including crimes against humanity. There were a total of 13 trials held at Nuremberg between 1945 and 1949. Those on trial included leading Nazis such as Hermann Goering, Hitler's chosen successor. Other Nazis faced trial elsewhere, including Rudolph Hoess, commandant of Auschwitz concentration camp, who signed this confession to confirm that he had ordered the murder of two million people. Hoess was executed in 1947.

LOOKING FOR CLUES

There are many physical reminders of the war present today, such as buildings and memorials. These have been built or preserved to remind people about the terrible events that took place between 1939 and 1945.

▶ *There are millions of photographs and other sources that tell the story of the war. Many of them are preserved in The National Archives and included in this book. This photo shows a Red Cross worker writing a letter home for an injured soldier.*

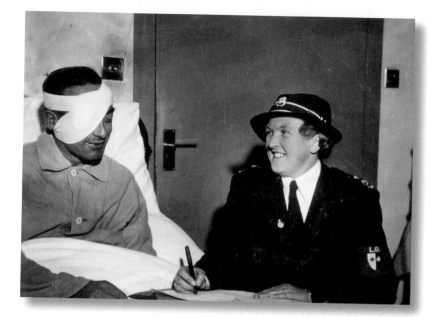

▼ *It can be hard to imagine the fierce battles fought on the peaceful beaches of Normandy. However, there are many reminders including gun emplacements, fortifications and memorials to those who died. In this picture, you can see the remains of one of the Mulberry harbours used in the invasion.*

► Beneath the streets of London, visitors can explore the underground bunker used by Winston Churchill and the British government during the darkest days of the war. The Map Room was constantly staffed throughout the war, mapping the progress of the Allied armies and navies around the world. This room is where Churchill met his ministers and generals while the bombs fell on London. The Churchill War Rooms are now a museum.

◄ This Memorial to the Murdered Jews of Europe stands in the centre of Berlin, Germany. It was opened in 1999, after Germany had been reunited. Its field of 2700 concrete slabs or 'stelae' are designed to represent the huge scale of the Holocaust. There are also memorials to other victims of the Nazis, such as the Roma people, homosexuals and the disabled.

► Auschwitz-Birkenau was the major centre for the murder of Jews and others during the war. Today, this death camp in Poland has been preserved as a World Heritage Site. According to UNESCO, part of the United Nations organization, the barbed wire, barracks and gas chambers of Auschwitz are a permanent symbol of "humanity's cruelty to its fellow human beings in the 20th Century".

WORLD WAR II TIMELINE

1939

23 August Nazi-Soviet Pact agreed between Hitler and Stalin, allowing Germany to invade Poland without being attacked by the Soviet Union.

1 September German troops invade Poland. Poland surrenders on 27 September.

3 September Britain and France declare war on Germany.

1940

9 April Germany begins invasion of Denmark and Norway.

10 May Germany invades Belgium and the Netherlands. German forces cross the French border on 12 May.

27 May Evacuation of 340,000 Allied soldiers from Dunkirk, France, begins.

10 June Italy joins the war as an ally of Germany.

22 June Armistice signed between Germany and France, giving Hitler's forces control of northern and western France, including Paris. A puppet government rules in the south.

13 August Battle of Britain begins over southern England, lasting until 15 September when Hitler abandons plans to invade Great Britain.

7 September Bombing raid on London marks the start of the Blitz on Britain.

27 September Germany, Japan and Italy agree the Tripartite Pact.

1941

22 June Start of Operation Barbarossa, Nazi invasion of the Soviet Union.

September Siege of Leningrad begins in Soviet Union.

7 December Japanese forces attack the US Navy base at Pearl Harbor, Hawaii, killing 2403 Americans. The United States declares war on Japan the next day. Germany and Italy declare war on the United States on 11 December.

1942

20 January At the Wannsee Conference, leading Nazis agree to carry out the systematic murder of millions of Jews in the Holocaust.

10 July American forces capture the island of Saipan after desperate Japanese resistance.

24 August Paris is liberated from German occupation.

1945

13-14 February Allied bombing of Dresden kills thousands of Germans in a firestorm, causing many people to question Allied bombing campaign.

19 February US Marines land on Japanese island of Iwo Jima, which is captured after fierce fighting.

30 April Death of Adolf Hitler.

8 May Victory in Europe (VE) day following surrender of Germany.

6 August Americans explode first atomic bomb at Hiroshima Japan, followed three days later by atomic bomb at Nagasaki.

15 August Emperor of Japan surrenders.

4 June The Battle of Midway begins, in which the United States wins a decisive victory over the Japanese fleet.

November Allied forces win a major victory at the Battle of El Alamein in North Africa. The Red Army launches a major offensive against German forces at Stalingrad.

1943

12 May Axis forces surrender in Tunisia, putting North Africa into Allied control.

5 July Battle of Kursk begins on Eastern Front, the largest land battle in history.

10 July Allied invasion of Sicily begins.

8 September Italy surrenders to the Allies, although German forces continue to fight in the country.

1944

21 January Allied forces land at Anzio, Italy, and attempt to capture Monte Cassino. The battle lasts for four months.

6 June D-Day landings on the beaches of Normandy.

Glossary

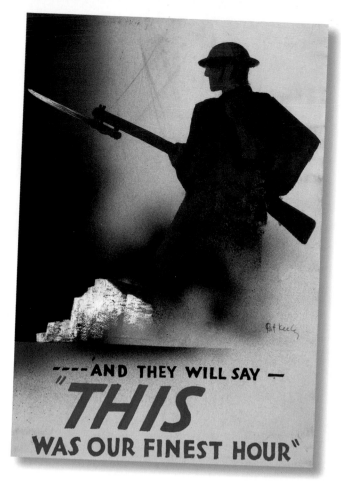

"----'AND THEY WILL SAY ---
"THIS
WAS OUR FINEST HOUR"

Allies countries fighting against Germany, Japan and the other Axis powers. After 1941, the Allies included Great Britain, the United States, the Soviet Union, Canada and many other countries

aristocrat member of a noble family

armistice agreement to end fighting in a war

Axis Germany, Japan, Italy (between 1940 and 1943) and their allies

capitalist economic and political system in which industries are controlled by private individuals rather than the state, generally with strong belief in individual freedom

colony land that is ruled from overseas, such as the colonies that made up the British Empire in 1939

communist economic and political system in which property and industries are controlled by the government, and everyone works for the state

conscription making it compulsory for people in a certain group to join the armed forces, such as all men between certain ages

convoy fleet of merchant ships accompanied by warships to protect them from attack

dictator ruler with no restrictions on their power, such as the possibility of being voted out of power. Hitler and Stalin were both dictators

double agent secret agent who is actually working for the organization or country they are supposed to be spying on

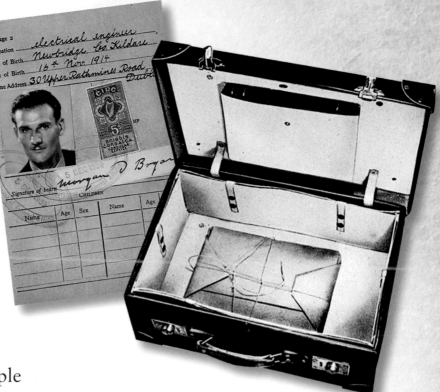

Holocaust the organised murder of millions of Jews and other people by the Nazis during World War II

incendiary type of bomb designed to start a fire

intelligence information gathered during wartime, often using secret agents or other hidden means

minefield area covered with hidden explosive devices called mines

misinformation information that is deliberately designed to mislead the enemy

neutral not involved in a war, and not favouring one side or the other

persecute singling out a person or group for harsh or unfair treatment

propaganda information designed to present a particular view, usually that of the government

puppet government government without much real power that has to follow the orders of another power, such as the government set up in southern France during World War II

sabotage deliberate damage to transport or other enemy facilities designed to disrupt military or political forces, such as blowing up railway lines

Soviet Union country made up of what are now Russia, Ukraine and several other countries. The Soviet Union broke up in 1991

FIND OUT MORE

Books

See Inside the Second World War by Rob Lloyd Jones and Maria Cristina Pritelli (Usborne, 2011)

Eyewitness: World War II (DK, 2014 edition)

True Stories of the Second World War by Paul Dowswell (Usborne, 2014)

History Relived: The Home Front by Cath Senker and Camilla Lloyd (Wayland, 2012)

Real Lives: Winston Churchill by Harriet Castor (A & C Black, 2012)

The Diary of a Young Girl by Anne Frank is an essential book for anyone who wants to understand what it was like to grow up hiding from the Nazis in occupied Europe.

There are many other fiction books about World War II that can give you an idea of what it was like to live through the events described in this book.

Online resources

The National Archives have created a fantastic online resource covering many aspects of World War II

http://www.nationalarchives.gov.uk/education/worldwar2/

The Imperial War Museum is home to a vast collection of artefacts and resources from the war. It's well worth a visit but you can also discover lots through the museum's website at **www.iwm.org.uk**

There are many other museums that tell the story of the war. Your local museum may explain how your home town was changed by the war. Other museums tell the story of certain aspects of the conflict, such as the National Army Museum. Find out more at **www.nam.ac.uk**

You can also find out more about other countries and how they remember the war. The Australian National War memorial website is a great place to find out about Australians' experiences in World War II **www.awm.gov.au/atwar/ww2/**

The United States Holocaust Memorial Museum includes lots of resources and information about the wartime persecution of Jews and others **www.ushmm.org**

𝒜 The National Archives

The National Archives is the UK government's official archive containing over 1,000 years of history. They give detailed guidance to government departments and the public sector on information management, and advise others about the care of historical archives.

www.nationalarchives.gov.uk

The National Archives picture acknowledgements and catalogue references

P5 DEFE 2/40 (2) D-Day War Diary 4 Commando 6 June 1944. P5 DEFE 2/499 D-Day, Mulberry B, looking SW 1944. P6 FO 96/221 No55 Handshakes for the Fuehrer at the Nazi Party Rally, Nuremberg 1933. P6 No53 Marching the flags at the Nazi Party Rally, Nuremberg 1933. P8 PREM 1/331A Telegram to Winston Churchill concerning Hitler's invasion of Poland, 1939. P9 PREM 1/266A The Munich agreement paper 30 September 1938. P9 FO 898/527 German troops occupy Poland 1939. P10 FO 898/527 French and British evacuees from Dunkirk 1943-19. P10 INF 3/1578 Air duel over crowded evacuation beach, Dunkirk Artist Bryan de Grineau 1939-1946. P11 INF 3/1436 (A) Hitler, with bloody sword, standing on France and contemplating invasion of England 1939-1946. P12 INF 1/244 Winston Churchill 1944-1944. P13 AIR 22/262 no 14387 RAF casualties 15 August 1940. P13 INF 1/244 Battle of Britain pilots and air gunners, possibly from a Defiant Squadron 1944-1944. P13 INF 1/264 Public morale, daily report 23 August 1940. P14 AIR 2/5238 Bombing of Coventry 1940. RDF stations 1940. P15 HO 193/1 Bomb Census map, East London 7-14 October 1940. P15 INF 2/44 London after the Blitz, St Paul's Cathedral 1944-1945. P15 FO 898/527 St Paul's Cathedral, London, obscured by smoke of bombs during the Blitz 1940. P16 KV 2/462 Edward Chapman (Zigzag) Chapman's ID card created by Nazi forgers 1941. P16 KV 2/862 Johann Jebsen anti-Nazi intelligence officer, British double agent code name Artist during the Second World War. P17 WO 208/4374 Juan Pujol-Garcia (codename Garbo) The Garbo network (written) World War II 1949-1949. P18 HW 25/3 Mathematical theory of ENIGMA machine by Alan Turing. P19 FO 850/234 Colossus electronic digital computer 1943. P21 EXT 1/48 Comrades in Arms (Churchill and Stalin) 1939-1945. P22 INF 13/213 World War II poster - The War Against Japan 1939-1945. P23 INF 3/791T Ditty Box Hitler boxer and Franklin Roosevelt Artist Wyndham Robinson 1939-1946. P24 INF 3/80 General Sir Bernard Montgomery 1939-1946. P24 PREM 3/109 Churchill to Wavell regarding the defence of Crete 28 April 1941. P25 WO 201/2846 Western Desert deception, dummy 25pdr gun made at Tobruk 1942. P25 DEFE 2/609 Operation Torch North Africa November 1942. P25 INF 3/1265 Grand Harbour, Malta, under air attack Artist Rowland Hilder 1939-1946. P26 KV 4/284 German sabotage chocolate bar 1942-1943. P27 MF 1/27 Locations of resistance groups and saboteurs in Northern Italy 1943-1945. P27 INF 2/7 French World War II poster - Salut A La Resistance 1945-1945. P28 HS 6/597 French resistance, arms deliveries by region 1942. P28 HS 7/49 Explosive rat 1941-1945. P29 HS 8/1032 SOE fake passport for Hitler p2 1941-1945. P29 HS 7/28 Incendiary Suitcase 1944. P30 ADM 205/30 New U-Boat bunker with bomb-proof roof at St Nazaire 9 December 1942. P31 MFQ 1/588 Allied merchant ships sunk in the Battle of The Atlantic, September 1939. P31 AIR 27/1568 U-570, first U-Boat captured by the British in WWII, surrenders to HMS Kingston Agate. P32 BT 131/40 Rationing Adult's Ration Book. P32 INF 3/225 Make do and mend Stuffed doll figure patching cloth 1939-1946. P33 MAF 102/15 War Cookery Calendar, May-June 1943-1952. P33 INF 13/140 World War II poster - Dig For Victory 1939-1945. P34 RAIL 1057/3280 Women war workers on railways 1939-1945. P35 INF 2/42 ATS girls plotting 1940-1943. P35 INF 13/140 World War II poster - Lend A Hand On The Land - Join The Women's Land Army. P35 INF 3/403 Women for Industry Women of Britain. Come into the factories Artist Zec 1939-1946. P36 INF 3/86 Evacuation of children Artist Showell 1939-1946. P36 HO 294/612 Czechoslovak Refugee Trust case papers (Kindertransport) 1938-1956. P37 DO 131/15 CORB children to New Zealand 1940-1941. P37 INF 14/12 Children learning to 'Dig For Victory'. P38 INF 3/137 War Effort and they will say this was our finest hour Artist Pat Keely 1939-1946. P39 DEFE 1/332 Postal and Telegraph Censorship Department worker checks the content of a letter 1939-1945. P39 KV 2/346 William Joyce (Lord Haw Haw) 1940-1946. P39 INF 2/37 Publicity material distributed from Cairo 1943-1949. P41 INF 2/3 World War II poster - Together 1943-1943. P41 WO 106/5921 Operation Mincemeat (The Man Who Never Was), ID card 1943. P41 WO 106/5921/4 Operation Mincemeat correspondence 1943. P42 INF 2/4 Avro Lancaster 1943-1944. P42 INF 2/43 Air Chief Marshal Sir Arthur T Harris 1944. P42 AVIA 53/627 Mr Barnes Wallis plans for bouncing bomb Operation Chastise Dambusters. P43 AIR 16/487 Bomber Command, accuracy of bombing of German cities graph 11, Oct 1945. P43 AIR 16/487 Bomber Command, devastation of German cities graph 10A, Oct 1945. P44 WO 205/173 Operation Titanic, dummy parachutists diversionary plan D-Day, 1944. P44 HW 1/2784 Ultra decrypt noting German observation of Operation Overlord May 1944. P45 HO 338/27 Troops climb through bomb damage debris, Caen 1944. P46 CN 11/8 Polish Jews stacking clothing 1942. P48 FO 371/30917 Reports of German plan to exterminate Jews August 1942. P49 FO 371/42806 Sketch of Auschwitz concentration camp by a former prisoner 1944. P49 HW 16/6 Part1 Intercept about the Holocaust September 1942. P50 NSC 5/96 Wings for Victory the Sky's the limit 1943. P50 FO 898/527 A boy surveys ruins in Warsaw, Poland 1943-1945. P51 CAB 106/1010 Nazi prisoners in Aachen October 1944. P51 CAB 106/1080 Surrender of all forces under German control signed at Berlin 8 May 1945. P51 AIR 20/4376 100-person Public Surface shelter at East India Dock Road, London, after flying bomb strike 4 August 1944. P52 INF 14/447 Yalta conference Churchill Stalin Roosevelt 1945. P53 INF 3/391 Anti-Japanese Posters Smash Japanese aggression RAF raid on Japanese flying boats Artist Roy Nockolds 1939-1946. P54 PREM 3/66/7 Stalin's tick on Churchill's note written at the Kremlin on 9 October 1944, dividing up the Balkans into spheres of influence 9 October 1944. P55 WO 309/217 Confession by Rudolf Hoess, Kommandant of Auschwitz, to the killing of two million prisoners of war 16 March 1946. P56 INF 2/43 Red Cross worker writing letter for wounded soldier 1939-1945.

INDEX

PICTURE ACKNOWLEDGEMENTS

Front cover: All images Shutterstock aside from the following: INF 3/403 Women for Industry Women of Britain, Come into the factories 1939-1946, Artist Zec. INF 1/244 Battle of Britain pilots and air gunners, possibly from a Defiant Squadron 1944-1944. INF 2/1 pt2 (516) Winston Churchill by Cecil Beaton 1939-1945. EXT 1/57 (2) World War II poster - Dig For Victory. INF 3/1571 Tank crew surrendering to British infantry, Artist Marc Stone. Press Agency photographer/Wikimedia.
Back cover: All images Shutterstock aside from the following: FO 96/221 No55 Handshakes for the Fuehrer at the Nazi Party Rally, Nuremberg 1933. HO 193/1 Bomb Census map, East London 7-14 October 1940. INF 3/80 General Sir Bernard Montgomery 1939-1946. INF 3/137 And they will say this was our finest hour, Artist Pat Keely 1939-1946. Mark Higgins/Shutterstock.
Inside images all Shutterstock aside from the following: p4 top 92424169 Roger Viollet/Getty Images, p4 bottom 488661231 PhotoQuest/Getty Images, p6 middle Ralf Roletschek/Wikimedia, p7 82139236 Paul Popper/Popperfoto/Getty Images, p8 bottom Brian C. Weed/Shutterstock, p9 top Right_Honourable_Neville_Chamberlain._Wellcome_M0003096/Wellcome/Wikimedia, p11 U.S. National Archives and Records Administration /Wikimedia, p13 top Paul Drabot/Shutterstock, p14 top Peteri/Shutterstock, p15 top U.S. National Archives and Records Administration/Wikimedia, p17 top 3395126 Kurt Hutton/Picture Post/Getty Images, p17 top right The National Archives INF3/267/Wikimedia, p18 top Mark Higgins/Shutterstock, p18 middle 520714001 Fine Art Images/Heritage Images/Getty Images, p19 top Antoine Taveneaux/Wikimedia, p20 Johannes Hähle/Wikimedia, p21 Max Alpert/RIA Novosti archive/image #543/Alpert /CC-BY-SA 3.0/Wikimedia, p23 top 106501480 Keystone-France/Getty Images, p23 middle U.S. National Archives and Records Administration/Wikimedia, p23 bottom U.S. National Archives and Records Administration/Wikimedia, p26 3424802G201 Three Lions/Getty Images, p31 U.S. Navy/Wikimedia, p33 3318150 Iava Katamidze Collection/Getty Images, p40 107759074 Galerie Bilderwelt/Getty Images, p43 118123779 Alinari Archives/Getty Images, p45 Archives Normandie 1939-45/Wikimedia, p46 170986804 Sovfoto/Getty Images, p47 500838679 Universal History Archive /Getty Images, p47 bottom Takkk/Wikimedia, p48 170980443 Sovfoto/Getty Images, p52 Hayakawa/Wikimedia, p53 top Charles Levy/Wikimedia, p53 middle US government photo/Wikimedia, p54 Robert Knudsen/Wikimedia, p55 United States Government/Wikimedia, p56 Bertl123/Shutterstock, p57 (top) Frankemann/Wikimedia, p57 (middle) Noppasin/Shutterstock, p57 (bottom) PlusONE/Shutterstock.